FINDING GOD

How I Got Here

K. E. Fagel

PAGE PUBLISHING
Conneaut Lake, PA

First originally published by Page Publishing 2024

ISBN 979-8-89315-172-5 (pbk)
ISBN 979-8-89315-191-6 (digital)

Printed in the United States of America

I dedicate this book to Diane. She was the driving force behind these beautiful changes in my life. I couldn't have done it without her.

Chapter 1

I was a middle-class White kid from divorced parents who cut his teeth in Vietnam for a year and spent the next forty years really pissed. I served with the 101st Airborne Ranger Unit L Co. in 1969 and 1970. My life had been filled with stress, anger, resentment, violence, dysfunction, sadness, and tremendous loss. I had been married and divorced three times and started over more times than Olympic sprinters in the gold medal one hundred-yard dash. Throughout my two years in the army and the last fifty-plus years since then, I have found and/or discovered some of the pieces to the puzzle of life, but not all of them by a long shot. Only recently have I found the way to peace, happiness, and true enlightenment by finding God.

I was diagnosed with PTSD (post-traumatic stress syndrome) in 1983, and I received treatment for it at the Cleveland VA under Dr. Walter Knake. I took part in the initial study done by Dr. Knake and Dr. Jon Wilson, who took the results of that study to Washington, DC, where the term stuck, and further study and support of this affliction of trauma began. It has been called many things over the years, like "battle fatigue," "shell shock," "soldier's heart," and "war neurosis." I attended group therapy sessions and spoke publicly in many different schools from middle school up to the college level. There were always a number of us Nam vets who went together with Dr. Knake. I also attended Dr. Knake's graduate psychology classes for eight years in order to help those students learn first-hand about PTSD and become better counselors. It didn't hurt that I have a bachelor of arts in psychology myself as well as a bachelor of science in biology. After this time, I began to speak publicly on my own and continued to do so until the early 2000s. I felt that if I could tell my story and reach one person, it was worth the price of rehashing old nightmares and memories of loss. I generally lose about three days after speaking because of those memories. The kids had no idea what Vietnam was anymore, so my efforts became futile. I had accumulated many letters of thanks from many students who I did touch, so the effort had been well worth it.

One story that stood out occurred at Shaker Heights Middle School in the 90s. I had taken some field equipment, a steel pot helmet, a rucksack, and a map of Vietnam. I asked for a volunteer to help me out and then picked a young man in the front before he could raise his hand. I said, "You're in the army now, boy!" It was divine intervention, as it turned out. The young man's name was Charles. I had already used the acronym "Charlie" in my presentation and then explained that it was not a derogatory term but a shortening of the words "Victor Charlie" from the military alphabet for "V" and "C." VC, of course, was the shortened version of Viet Cong and stated as VC or Victor Charlie on all radio communications. Charlie understood, so we proceeded to put on the field gear, rucksack, and steel pot helmet without further gear, and Charlie was reaching his carrying limit. He was beginning to understand just how hard all of this must have been. We generally carried about one hundred pounds. Charlie was a great sport, and he did very well.

After the class, Charlie asked for my autograph, and as I gave it to him, I asked him to tell his dad, Welcome home. He'd told me his dad and uncle served in Nam. He said his dad passed away. He had broken down under the stress of Vietnam and committed suicide! I was crushed! Regrouping, I told him to tell his uncle, Welcome home. Charlie then said that he, too, had passed away for the same reason. For a moment, I thought I had failed, but I was wrong. Charlie connected with me, and like a grown man, he understood and told me, "Welcome home." As bad as I felt, I was tearing up just writing this. I knew I had done a good thing for Charlie. God bless him. He is so brave. He, in turn, gave me what I needed—the validation that I was doing the right thing. I hope Charlie always remembers me. I know I'll always remember him.

Chapter 2

Shortly after I turned sixty, I was diagnosed with congestive heart failure. I had many spinal issues, many procedures, and several surgeries over the last eight years, and they had all taken their toll. Being really pissed all these years was more than likely the cause of the heart failure. I was going through a real rough patch. I had recently filed for divorce, my third one, and all was crashing down around me. That divorce was another story I won't delve into here. It was a real doozy, though.

I left the town of Antlers, Oklahoma, where I had a horse ranch, to visit my brother in Charlotte, North Carolina. When I got there, I found out that our dad had just passed away. We set out for upstate New York, via Cleveland, to pick up my daughter. We all spent about five or six days there and took care of business. When I returned to Cleveland, I was in bad shape. Somehow, I managed to rent a small house, move in, and get appointments at the VA. Long story short, I went to the emergency room one Friday night because I could barely breathe, sleep, eat, or essentially do anything. "Congestive heart failure," the doctor said.

"You have the wrong patient!" I said. He told me that I had about a week to live. He had given me a diuretic and said I'd be peeing like a race horse, and good luck getting home with dry pants. I had about fifty pounds on me that didn't belong there. I did start getting some relief, and I did get home with dry pants, but at the same time, it was pretty scary. I had a lot to learn. I committed myself to the process and learned all I could. I went to the heart clinic at the VA, saw my primary care doctor (what a hack), read all I could, and used the health buddy system for recording daily numbers and getting good advice. My diet was always good, but I became more aware of the salt content of processed foods, fast foods, and restaurant food. It wasn't easy, but it was necessary if I wanted to survive. That wasn't even a question for me.

In a few months, I was at my normal weight of 185 pounds. I was walking over a mile every day, working out on the BowFlex, and swimming. I was starting to get my life back. I was also learning how to let go of the past and be in the present moment. I was learning how not to react to stressors and just accept things as they are. That was a tough one. I was anxious about a few things, and one morning I was getting ready to go for a walk. I was folding some clothes I just took out of the dryer, and I became really hot and sweaty. I was nauseous and fainted. My heart rate was over 105, and I didn't know why. I had taken all my meds. I wasn't upset or anxious, yet I felt like I was going to keel over. I chewed two aspirins and laid down. Within a few minutes, my heart rate slowed down, and I was feeling normal. I admitted to myself how much I missed my three daughters and how much it hurt. I let all that emotion out, and I began to heal. I was amazed. For once, I didn't get angry and carried on. I began learning that lesson on that day. Admitting how I felt instead of getting angry about the situation slowed down my heart rate and prevented me from doing any more damage.

Chapter 3

I tried many methods to find peace and happiness in my life, but I was still struggling with the inability to totally succeed. I had acquired some wealth a couple of times in my life and lost it all both times. I had many possessions and toys, but I found that nothing could bring me peace and happiness except for horses. I was then in no shape to have horses in my life. It was a shame too, because I always wanted to be a cowboy. I have a picture of me on horseback when I was about four years old. My mom wrote on it, "This is where it all started." She was right too. Some of the methods I tried were isolation in the Rocky Mountains in Colorado, spiritual readings, meditation, and various techniques related to *The Secret*. Some things worked for a while, but they never lasted. I realized that I was at a crossroads in my life, and the next choice I made would be profound.

I started studying Eckhart Tolle and the philosophy of enlightenment through awakening. Once I had wrapped my head around the concept of awakening, it did not take long to apply it to my life. All the things that caused me stress or a negative reaction became a test for me to become enlightened. There were so many stressors in my life that I had many to choose from. With a philosophy like this, which is so intricate and so critical to use in all moments of our lives in order to succeed, I realized that I could start anywhere in my life with those things that caused me stress and begin to move in the right direction. I chose to apply the technique of "being in the now" or "being in the present moment." I became aware of all my reactions to outside stimuli. I asked myself how I could handle those situations better. I thought of being transparent about it all. I started recognizing the stimuli but did not have a reaction to them or an opinion about them. I found that doing that created a space between dysfunction and peace of mind, or just "being.' The greater the space created, the greater the peace of mind or awareness of "being" became. As I continued to learn this philosophy, I applied it to more situations in my life.

One day, after an afternoon out and doing very well with all the things that normally cause me to react, I returned home to a loud dirt bike, racing up and down the street, and blurted out how I would "run that damn kid over, back up, and run him over again." I had lost touch with all the positive, nonreactive behaviors and immediately digressed back into my pain. I just had to revive it. My ego was threatened by this new way. I knew that I had to get past this and stop reacting to outside stimuli. I had to remember that I have PTSD, and loud, sudden noises are a huge trigger. For a split second, I thought I was being attacked and that I had to react. PTSD controls me, not the other way around. I had to work harder and just be. It's a hard concept to perceive, isn't it?

Driving has always been a stressor for years, and congestion on the roads has really created many reactions from me in the last forty years. My vehicle was like a weapon, and other vehicles were the enemies. If I got cut off, slowed down, or even flipped off, it was game on. I then had to try to think differently. Yeah, I know. Good luck with that. I tried to think only of the moment when I got in my truck and not the final destination. When I focused on the present moment, I had no thoughts of how future events would unfold. Therefore, I had no stress about future events and found that I enjoyed the present moment even more. I continued to look at every step in the process and remembered that complete enlightenment happens over time, and I was moving in that direction. I took the good out of what I had accomplished and made note of the things that still needed work without judging or being critical. Every day, I reinforced the good that came from this practice and continued to work at it. As always, there are good days and bad days. The bad days are not nearly as bad, and the good days are really good.

Chapter 4

It's been about three years now since I started reading the Bible. I wish I had started much sooner, but I guess life got in the way. My Bible was from the 50s, and it was small and hard to read, so I bought a new one. Written in it is a method on how to read the Bible in one year. I felt like it was a good idea and very doable, so I got started. There were so many things I wanted to learn, and I didn't really know where to start, so that seemed like a great way to begin. The story is really incredible and very detailed, and I knew that it would take more than one read, so I came up with a two-part plan: (1) read the book from start to finish, and (2) look up specific questions and learn those points of interest. There is a list of different subjects and the scriptures to read at the back of the book with regard to that subject matter. I read the book in ten months and learned quite a bit, but the more I learned, the more questions I had. I became more interested in what other people perceived when reading the Bible, and by God's will, I started meeting some pretty incredible and knowledgeable people. They all had a certain way about them that was very kind and loving. They didn't swear, curse, or speak negatively about anyone. I thought, *Geez, aren't we supposed to call out sinful behavior and use cursing to exemplify it?* I spent the better part of my adult life doing that! My dad always said that I had every right to be mad, but I realized that it came out of my own hide.

When I found the scripture that said not to curse and forgive our neighbors, I remembered looking up as if speaking to God and saying, "Lord, I know you know my neighbor!" I didn't see the big picture. As I continued to read, I learned that we need to forgive others as we would like to be forgiven. That was one of the first things I started to work on. In the process, I started using different words to express my emotions rather than cursing. I found out how important it was to pray, so I learned how to do that also. I learned that we need to have a close relationship with God and Jesus, so I started talking to them both and took them with me wherever I went. I started to change. I started asking specifically for what I wanted and got it. When I went to the store, I asked God to make sure my favorite parking spot was open, and if everything on my list was on the shelf, that would be great. If I needed gas, I would say, "Lord, if I could pull up to an empty pump and not have to wait, that would be great." Some of the people I met were as critical to my learning process as the reading. I heard incredible, miraculous stories and thought, *Hmmm, can I do that?* Then I read what Jesus said: "Ask the Lord for what you want and need in my name, and you shall receive it." I began to realize that we all had the same playbook, and it was up to us to learn and live by God's word.

Chapter 5

Being born in 1950, I grew up in a very different world than what we have today. The war was over for five years, and prosperity was a new way of life. There were two chickens in every pot and a car in every drive. The men went back to work, and the women went back to raising the families. Television was soon to be on the market, so we wanted more forms of entertainment. We played outside all day, and baseball was a big favorite. It was America's sport, played by all. A bat and a ball, or a stick and a rock, were all we needed. Going outside and playing with anything is how it was done. We didn't need a few hundred dollars for gear and a ride to the park. The world was our playground, and it felt like it every time we went outside. We owned the outdoors. We were all red-faced, red-blooded American kids out for yet another adventure in the wild outdoors. What would we tame or conquer today? It was a leave-it-to-beaver life for the most part, where children were to be seen and not heard, and we didn't dare talk back. We went to school and church, and we ate dinner as a family every night. Our elders were to be respected and obeyed. I loved playing baseball, biking, and fishing. I learned to swim at an early age and really loved learning to water ski. My Uncle Bob taught me to ski, and it took about seventeen tries before I got up, but each time, he'd pull back around and ask if I was okay. "Yes, sir," I replied. He never got impatient, and it was just what I needed to learn. I got pretty good at riding my bike and won first place in our school rodeo.

Chapter 6

My parents were from Schenectady, New York, just south of the Adirondack Mountains. General Electric (GE) grew really big during the war, making bombs, and my mother, father, and aunt all worked there. My dad went to Union College, so we lived in a college housing development built specifically for this purpose. They were two-bedroom bungalows, and the development was still under construction, so there were some very cool spots for us to play there. We were a family of four and lived like many people at that time. My perspective was that of a very young boy and younger brother, so I had to learn how the game was played, when I could talk, and what I could do on my own. It didn't always work out, as most kids learn from their mistakes.

My brother Johnny and I had pet turtles—those little paint turtles, which were cheap and replaceable. Each week, the bowl had to be cleaned, so we'd put them in the tub with fresh water while cleaning the bowl. One week, I was waiting for Mom to finish the ironing so I could help out, and it seemed to drag on forever. I went impatiently to nudge Mom into the bathroom. My attempt failed, so I waited in the bathroom for her to finish. It seemed like a couple of weeks went by, but the sun was still up, so I guessed not. Then I got an idea, and I thought I'd look like a really good boy doing chores without needing any help and making Mom happy. I mean, I was right there next to the faucets. I knew how to turn them on, so I proceeded to do so. The turtles were in the tub already, so what was I waiting for? I called once more for Mom, and when she didn't respond, I took that to mean that I should go ahead. So I leapt into adulthood, and I turned on the faucet and watched the tub slowly fill with water. I was so proud, and I didn't need any help. As the tub filled, the turtles scurried away from the water. I thought that maybe they didn't want a bath. Wrong! As the water reached the turtles, they were slowly scalded by the steaming water. I turned on the wrong faucet! So much for adulthood!

Chapter 7

My dad worked for GE after college with a master's in chemistry. In 1956, at the age of five, we moved to Cleveland, Ohio. We did not know anyone. There were no other family members there. Most of the people we knew worked at GE or went to the same church. Almost everyone was pretty much the same, so it wasn't too hard to adjust. Children were to be seen and not heard. You never disrespected your parents. God's rule is to honor thy mother and father, so we obeyed no matter what. We all went to church every Sunday, had Sunday school, and read the Bible after dinner. We ate together as a family every night. TV shows reflected family values with good, wholesome entertainment. It didn't hurt that I looked like Beaver Cleaver. We all played outside and went to the park or school for pickup games or just plain goofing around. These days, it's called "hanging out." *Gunsmoke* was in its second season and soon became the most popular and longest-running show on TV. The reason was that it was realistic. The mid- to late-1800s reflected the times of a new country, a civil war that pitted family against family (nothing civil about it), abolished slavery, and pioneered the West. As one group of people were freed, the dissemination of another continued, along with the near extinction of the buffalo.

The year I was in the fifth grade, my parents had just divorced. Life got really hard after that because divorce was frowned on, and I lost all my friends because of it. My friends at school, church, and in the neighborhood all rejected me. I didn't understand why I was being punished because of what my parents did. Society had a lot of influence then when it came to social norms, and I didn't like it at all. That was really the beginning of me spending many years being very angry at everybody and everything. I felt excluded from everything.

I didn't get to play Little League until the divorce, and when I did, I excelled to become the best player on the team that year. At the end of the season, when the all-star team was picked, I finally felt like things were turning around. Then it was announced in front of the entire team that I was not eligible to play because I hadn't collected enough money. I was shocked. Who would make such a silly rule? My mom felt the same way because she read the manager the riot act in front of everyone. It crushed me because I realized that nothing had changed.

The all-star game was played at Forest Hills Park, and it was a beautiful, sunny day. I stayed hidden in the tree line behind the outfield and watched as the team got ready for the game. My friend and teammate, Michael J., saw me and came out to greet me. He didn't know what to say. Finally, he told me that what they did to me was shameful. "Kenny, you are the best player on this team, and today's game means nothing because you aren't in it!" I thanked him and then turned around and left. I tried to put into perspective all the things that were taken from me and how I was supposed to deal with them. I couldn't, so I became angry. My parents were divorced. I lost all my neighborhood friends. I felt like I was banned from playing baseball, and I did not know where to turn. My older brother, Johnny, was anything but a good brother. He was playing baseball at school and in the Pony League in the summer, and he was quite good. He could hit like Babe Ruth. I decided to take another crack at it in the seventh grade, and I had a lot of fun. I remember being up at the plate for this one at bat, and a kid behind the backstop yelled out, "Hit it like your brother, Kenny!" I looked back. The pitch was thrown, and as I turned to see the pitch, I swung wildly and struck out. All I heard was booing.

Chapter 8

Ike was president at the time and was very popular. He created interstate highways, having learned from his experience in WWII. He was really good at building infrastructure where there was nothing. He came to Cleveland one day, and my mom made arrangements to see him downtown. Ike and his popularity meant nothing to me; I was a kid! I came home for lunch every day, but not this day. What the heck! Where was I going to find food? I came home. Mom was there, and I got fed. Now what? She told me that I was going to my friend's house. His mom would feed me, and she would be home after school. Phew! I was not going to starve! So I came home after school, and my mom was bouncing off the walls! OMG! She was so excited. I got to see him really close, and he shook my hand and smiled at me. I thought I peed my pants a little, and I couldn't quite get any words out that I remembered. I would never EVER, EVER, EVER wash my hand again! OMG! I touched IKE. He shook my hand, and he said hi. Oh my god! I didn't know squat about women yet, but I learned later on that this was a state of mind you could not reason with. If you think I just implied that I knew squat about women, forget it. I don't. Do I look like an idiot?

Ike, bikes, lifestyle, air raids, cold war, divorce, social stigma, life changes, and challenges—anger develops over many small things.

Chapter 9

I was hurt on the job back in 1991. I broke my back, and much later I found out that I also broke my neck. I was using a core drill to make holes for rail posts on a loading dock. I had used the drill all morning with no problems. It worked just fine. Just after lunch, I started again and first made sure that the drill stand was secured to the concrete floor and the compressor was on. The first time the drill bit got stuck in the concrete, the base gave way and started spinning around the bit. It hit my feet, knocked me right on my ass (thus breaking my back), and then came around again and hit me in the head. I put my left arm up to block the blow, but its force threw me some thirty feet on the cold, hard, filthy concrete. As I was laying there in agony, my helper walked in and said, "Ken, lying down on the job," in the tone of Tim, the copy man from *Saturday Night Live*. It was actually funny. If you saw the show, you'd get it.

I was laid up for five weeks and had to stay in bed to let the injuries heal. I got back on my feet slowly, began to exercise, and then worked out lightly until I could handle more. I thought I was pretty much healed, and the only symptom I had was that when I sneezed or coughed, both arms went completely numb for a couple of seconds. Since it was such a short time, what should I complain about or to who? I discovered a chiropractor a few years later, and he cared for me and fixed me whenever my back flared up. It seemed to have a mind of its own, but as it turned out, that mind was me. More on that later.

I had some real debilitating back issues in 1998, so I went to a doctor for treatment, and I was told that I had spinal stenosis, a couple bad discs, and the pain was from inflammation. I was given prednisone, and in a few days, I blew up like a balloon. I had never been so uncomfortable before in my life. I was unsuccessful at getting any more information from the doctor, but I was sent to physical therapy. That worked out fairly well for a while, and then I became frustrated with the lack of progress. This was when I found a chiropractor and got his opinion on what the source of pain might be. I was warned by the therapist that chiropractors were quacks, but I really did not believe him. After an hour of examining me, the doctor told me he was 90 percent sure that he knew what was wrong and 100 percent sure that he could fix it. I asked when he could start, and he said that if I had time, he could start in fifteen minutes. Off came the back brace, and I lay down on the exam table and waited. I walked out forty-five minutes later, standing erect with no back brace and no pain. My sacroiliac was out of joint, and it created a lot of inflammation. I stopped taking the prednisone, and the weight dropped right off. It wasn't until 2003 that a small car accident exacerbated these injuries. But, boy, did it ever! I was coming home from a friend's around 11:00 p.m., and I was on a dirt road on a horse ranch in the mountains in Colorado, and I skidded on the washboards in the road, turned sideways, and plowed through a metal horse fence. I hit my head on the windshield, the airbag deployed, and I basically got the shit kicked out of me. I couldn't remember my name. The problem was that, a few days later, I still couldn't remember my name.

Chapter 10

A few weeks later…you guessed it. I couldn't remember my name. I went to Denver VA for six months and got dicked around with more bullshit than you can believe. The physical therapist who started to treat me pulled her hands back and said, "I can't touch you. You'll have to go back to the doctor." Unbelievable, screwing with a guy in that condition who couldn't remember his name. That was just wrong.

I went to a local doctor for an unrelated rash, and he took one look at me and asked, "What's wrong with your neck?" I was sent for an MRI the next day and was given the names of three neurosurgeons for a review of the film. I called one of the doctors after I got the MRI done and made an appointment. The office gal said that it would be three weeks before they could see me unless it was an emergency, then it would be right away. About an hour later, I got a call from the doctor's office, and they asked if I could come in the next day at 9:30 a.m.

I said, "Wow, that's great service…uh…wait a minute, that's not good is it?"

"Well, we'll see you then," she said.

I had some experience reading films from various veterinary jobs I had, and although I was no expert, I could read some basic stuff. I stopped to pick up the film the next morning before the appointment, and as I took out the first picture, I saw my spinal cord looking like an hourglass at C-6 and C-7, and then I gasped for breath. "Oh, man. I am screwed!" Sure enough, five doctors later, I was screwed! I told you I could read some basic stuff, and being screwed was as basic as it got. The surgery couldn't be done for thirty days!

They told me that I could trip up a step and be paralyzed for life—quadriplegic. Once I was fixed, however, the symptoms would all go away. The disc burst inward and compressed the spinal cord. Removing the disc would take the pressure off, and the spinal cord would resume its normal shape. The one-hour ride home back up the mountain to 8,300 feet was excruciatingly scary. Anything could happen. I made it safe and sound. I did not leave the first floor for thirty days. Then I took another excruciatingly scary ride back down the mountain. Once I was in the hospital, I was a calm mountain stream because I now knew that I would be fixed. This was essentially the beginning of my journey through extreme pain, discomfort, misery, and torture and, at the same time, the beginning of the formation of my new wings. I would go on to have many more surgeries, procedures, tests, and even more surgeries before I would begin to see that light very clearly for the first time.

Chapter 11

During this time of pain and isolation, I had the opportunity to observe all the wonders of nature in the Rocky Mountains, and it all came to my doorstep—deer, elk, fox, bear, mountain lions, eagles, hawks, hummingbirds galore, and more. I began taking pictures and videos that just astounded me. I was occupied to the point of dropping everything for a great picture. One morning, I was on the drive in the snow, barefoot and wrapped in a towel (just got out of the shower), taking a video of a herd of elk. I was surrounded by this extreme beauty, and I did not even notice that I was standing barefoot in the snow, twenty degrees in the Rockies in the middle of winter. Okay, it was a sunny day, but still!

The eight years I was there were an epiphany to me because I had come to know the secret of nature. I had a wolf and seven horses. Every day, a herd of elk and deer came through the yard, just feet away from the house. I learned to truly understand nature, not just know how it works—balance in all things in nature and the evolution of a species in all of nature and in all things. I fully believe that we are all part of the same thing. We are the same, moving among what we perceive to be different but are in actuality the same thing— energy. It is up to us to find that balance in life that is God-given and to work each day to maintain that balance. It is up to us to perceive that balance must be achieved to be fully enlightened. All things are lessons toward achieving the same goal—becoming one with all things—becoming one with God. Some may call it the universe or a higher power, but I call it God.

Humankind has always tried to convey its thoughts, ideas, and feelings by using symbols of some kind, almost always falling short of some kind of universal understanding of it all. From cave drawings of the crudest nature to ancient texts in many forms, artworks in many forms, writings, and teachings, man has tried to convey as best he could all things perceived as epiphanies. A life-changing event or understanding of some facet of life that makes you think, "Wow! I finally get it. It's been right there all along." I was raised to believe that if you want something, you have to fight for it. It's a dog-eat-dog world, so to speak, but sometimes we have to fight our inner selves to get what we want. You want a job done, right? Do it right yourself. I soon learned that no man does anything alone. So what does it really mean when you say, Do it yourself? I believe that if you know how to do an actual job and not just tell others how to do it, respect will be earned, and those doing the job will do it better. Leading by example, so to speak. So keeping the balance means putting the time in to learn a job, but knowing that it takes a team to be truly productive, delegating work as a manager is essential for overall production.

As I started looking for balance in all things in my life, I began to work on the simple things like driving, shopping, going to the post office, and anything that put me in a crowd, a line, or a cluster. I forgot why those things made me anxious and looked at how to balance the stress. Would I be stuck in traffic all day? Probably not. Would I be in a line all day and be inconvenienced in some way? Probably not. As long as I chose when and where I went, some places were less crowded than others—less risk, less stress. I would be darned if it didn't make a significant difference. I was soon able to go to multiple stops and do multiple chores without feeling like I'd be ambushed, attacked, or otherwise forced to go covert into guerilla warfare.

Chapter 12

I was in the tenth grade when Mom came up to my third-floor bedroom that I shared with my stepbrother Bill. She had bad news. Our good friend and neighbor, Fred West, was killed in Vietnam. He was a marine and a very good young man. We went to his funeral a couple of days later, and the casket was closed. I didn't know what to think about what just happened, let alone a runaway imagination over a closed casket. Fred came to our house shortly before he left for Vietnam. He was in his dress uniform and so proud to be serving his country. Our parents "saved the world" in WWII, so they and the government felt it was our duty to fight in Vietnam under the guise of slowing the spread of communism. A young songwriter named Arlo Guthrie wrote a song called "Alice's Restaurant" about that time. A few lyrics went like this: "Well it's 1, 2, 3 what are we fighting for. Don't ask me I don't give a damn. Next stop is Vietnam. It's 5, 6, 7 open them pearly gates. It ain't no use to wonder why. Whoopie we're all gonna die!" This song has played on FM radio every Thanksgiving. The song was quite long, maybe eighteen minutes. Arlo told the story about going to the draft board with the idea of being rejected, so when asked why he wanted to join up, he replied, "to kill. I want to kill." His effort failed.

It was known that Ho Chi Minh wanted to unite North and South Vietnam, much like we did in the civil war. He came to President Eisenhower for help and was declined. He went to Russia's Khrushchev next. He was all in. Basically, it was the US vs. Russia. The only difference was that Russia only supplied the weapons. The war for us started in 1965. The war in Vietnam started one hundred years before this time. No one living there had ever seen a day of peace.

The next two years, after Fred died in 1966, were full of imaginative thoughts about Vietnam. A group of us got together and organized a war game that took place in residential Shaker Heights. There were two teams, and the goal was to capture and return to the base as many enemy combatants as possible. To say that it was a blast was to put it mildly. Sneaking around a populated area, staying hidden, and seeking out our enemy were a real rush. I wondered if this was what Vietnam was like. There was no time for wondering. I might get captured, and I didn't want that. A few hours passed with no captures, and it was getting late, so my buddy Gary and I went back to the base. There we met three opposing team members, and they told us that the game was over and they'd take us back to our car. After all, these were our buddies in real life too, so we had no reason to doubt them. Too bad; we should have. They took us to the Shaker Heights transit tracks, made us lie on the track, and then bombed us with eggs. As they drove away laughing, we wondered what the heck just happened. It was a five-mile walk back to the car, and we smelled like rotten eggs all the way. When I got home, my parents were having a Sunday dinner party, and to say that they were pissed at what I'd done and how I looked and smelled was putting it mildly. I learned a huge lesson that day—DON'T GET CAUGHT, EVER!

During those two years, I did a lot of fighting. Looking back, I was going through all this in order to prepare for war. I didn't think there was going to be another option, so I prepared for war.

Chapter 13

After I graduated high school in 1968, I went to Miami Beach with a friend named Joel. We stayed at the Beau Rivage, which was right on the beach, and it was beautiful. Joel and I would go down to the pool and hang out for the first couple of days, and it was like a piece of heaven. One morning, we saw two other fellas, and they came up to us and started chatting. Rich Davies and his friend were nice enough, and we got along fine. At one point, Rich Davies told us that they were hotel hopping and asked if they could crash with us for a couple of days. Joel and I had no problem with that, so we took them up to the room and returned to the pool. A couple in their thirties warned us that these guys might be ripping us off. They said that there was a lot of that going on. I kind of laughed and said we didn't have anything to take, and we weren't worried. We went down to the beach and had a blast body surfing, strolling up and down, and watching everybody play. I saw the most gorgeous young lady I had ever seen before, and in spite of being bashful and having little experience with girls or gorgeous women, I walked right up to her and invited her to come out dancing with all of us that night. Her name was Beverly North, and I was smitten.

We all went out to a couple of nightclubs and had an absolute ball. We danced, had a couple of drinks, danced some more, and then went back to the hotel. We stayed up late and talked about everything, sharing stories with our newfound pals. We all crashed late that night and slept like babies, with a light breeze from the ocean blowing in from our second-floor balcony. The next morning, as we were getting ready to go back down to the beach, the bellhop brought me a telegram. It was from my mom. She said that my dog, Duke, was killed by a car. I was stunned. He was my first and only dog, and I loved him very much. Rich saw that I was stressed, and he asked what was wrong. I said, "My dog died." Rich suggested that they all give me some alone time and proceeded to go down to the beach. I joined them some time later and never said another word.

We all went back to the room late in the afternoon and chilled out for a while. The balcony doors were half open, as were the curtains. Joel, Rich, his friend, and Beverly were all there with me, and I just got the strangest feeling that something was on the balcony. Being on the second floor, it was not like anyone had access to the room, but I got up and looked anyway. Nothing! Another few minutes went by, and I felt it again. Someone or something was on the balcony. I got up and looked again. Nothing! As I sat back down on the bed, a flash of light came flying into the room from the balcony and out the door to the hallway. Joel and I jumped up and ran to the hallway, looking up and down. Nothing! What the heck did we just see? We walked back into the room and asked if anybody saw that. Yes. They all did. Rich started to tell me that it was okay. That flash of light was his deceased uncle, an avid pet lover, with my deceased dog. I was stunned and had no idea what to think. Rich proceeded to tell me a complete description of my dog, including his name. Keep in mind that all I said was "my dog had died." Rich said that he was hit by a car, and he came here to let me know that he was alright and not to worry. I have a strong belief in the spiritual world, so I didn't doubt what I saw or heard for a minute, but how did Rich know?

Chapter 14

The next few days were like the first few activities, and we were driving around the beach area the next morning when "Born to Be Wild" came on the radio by Steppenwolf. It was number 17 on the pop charts. Rich said that by Friday (it was then a Tuesday), that song would be number 1. Nobody thought that it was even a remote possibility. Oh, ye of little faith. On Friday morning, the DJ did the countdown and then said, "The song we've all been waiting for, 'Born to Be Wild' by Steppenwolf, is number 1 on the hits chart. Whaaat! How did he do that?"

Two days later, Joel was going home, but I was staying a bit longer and then going to my brother's wedding in Brooksville, Florida. We were sitting on the beds, all of us, and Rich said to Joel, "There's something wrong with your girlfriend. She's lying in bed and not feeling well." Joel never said one word about having a girlfriend. He didn't have any pictures and never mentioned her name in any regard. We were all at the point where, when Rich said he "knew" something, he knew it. Joel immediately picked up the phone and called his girlfriend. Rich said, "Nancy is in her bed and seems to be having discomfort in her neck."

Joel said, "Nancy, Nancy, Nancy, are you alright?"

"Oh, Joel," said Nancy, "I don't feel well."

Rich then said, "Her neck is all red, and it has something to do with the sun."

Nancy told Joel that they'd been at the beach all day, and her neck was badly sunburned. Rich then told Joel that she was wearing her favorite nighty. When Joel asked what she was wearing, Nancy said, "Oh, Joel, you pervert. I'm wearing my favorite nighty!"

Joel fell off the bed, dropped the phone, and screamed, "I'm coming home! I'm coming home! Don't go anywhere!" Not one word was said about Nancy, not even her name, yet Rich knew it all.

After my brother's wedding, I traveled to Skokie, Illinois, to visit Rich, his family, and friends. As I got off the plane and was walking toward the terminal, there was a large crowd of people with balloons and signs that said, "Welcome to Chicago, Kenny." I started looking around for Kenny Rogers, thinking he must have been on the plane. I walked up to Rich, greeted him, and said that someone famous named Kenny was on the plane. He laughed and said, "No, no, no, that's for you. These are all my friends." Wow.

Chapter 15

Looking back at the heart issues and the decisions I faced, I found that I continued to move forward and make better choices all the time. I got new insurance in 2012 after making little progress at the VA in 2011. I got a new doctor at the Cleveland Clinic. I worked on artificial organs in the 70s as a fabricator. Another man and I built an artificial heart that broke the world's record for the longest pumping device. My doctor was enamored with my experience and asked me to tell him and his interns some stories from back then. I told him that the clinic was one building, and we worked across the street, behind a gas station in a warehouse with no windows.

When the record was broken, the world threw money at the clinic, and it became what it is today. I felt comfortable going there. I was examined, tested, and treated well for the first time. I was advised to get a defibrillator/pacemaker implant to help regulate my heart rate when and if I had a problem. Things could change fast when anything made the heart work harder. My problem was inefficient pumping from the left ventricle at about 25 percent and that caused the heart to work more to try and catch up. When it couldn't catch up, it caused your body to make you fall down and land on your head until you got it. I had a hard time agreeing to this implant for many reasons. In all my previous surgeries, I was on my stomach and never had to look at the doctor. With this one, I'd be on my back and not fully anesthetized. I did not want to accept that I couldn't correct this problem. I didn't want any more surgeries. I was at twenty-five and counting, and out of that twenty-five, one was a foot surgery, another was a knee surgery, and the other was a neck surgery. That meant twenty-three back surgeries. Enough!

I kept remembering what Dr. Kang said: "Ken, this is not an emergency (remember that last word?), but I would recommend the surgery sooner rather than later." When he suggested doing this in two months, I thought, *How the hell is THAT later?* Back to that last word, "emergency," I felt very strongly that there was an unspoken message there. Maybe there were three choices: sooner, later, or right now, dummy! I wrestled with the decision, and I labored and finally called the heart doctor, Dr. Lee. He said in all honesty that if this was him, he would do it now, so I should keep the appointment. I felt that it was quite profound because they didn't make that kind of statement very often anymore. Too many people take it literally. It's weird, isn't it? We need the doctors to tell us what to do, but they can't tell us anymore, so we have to read in between the lines. Now there's a leap, damn lawyers!

I did have the implant done in March of 2012, and it went well. The only time I was knocked out was at the end, when they tested it. I had no idea what that was like, but I was going to find out. I recovered nicely and started slowly getting my metal back. After about three months, I received a call from the device department telling me that the device just paid for itself. I asked how that was, and they told me that I had an episode the night before, and the device shocked me back into a normal heart rhythm during my sleep. I did not know how I missed that. I was speechless and trying to process what it all meant. Had I not gotten the implant, I would very likely be dead. Thank you, Lord, for leading me and not giving up on me.

Chapter 16

I have been a huge baseball fan since the early 50s, as long as I can remember. Baseball is a true reflection of life, and many lessons can be learned about life through baseball. "Never quit" comes to mind. I love Yogism. Those are cockeyed sayings made famous by Yogi Berra, the famous New York Yankees catcher. "It ain't over till it's over" is how Yogi expressed never quitting. "Nobody goes there anymore; it's too crowded." "It's déjà vu all over again." "You get cash, which is just as good as money." His unique way of expressing these quips was well-loved, understood, and long since made famous by the affable ball player. There is only one perfect game pitched in a World Series, and it was by Don Larson. Yogi called every pitch and caught the entire game. There have been twenty-four perfect games pitched, and the last one was by Domingo 'German in 2023 a Yankee.

I have accumulated a lot of trivial information over the years of watching many games at many levels, and there is nothing else I can compare to baseball that doesn't happen in life. So much of this game is implied in the form of strategy, and not so subtle trickery is pushed to the limit. How much of an advantage can be gained by this trickery, and how far can it go? There are strict rules, but not all of them are written. If both teams do it, the game is being played within its boundaries. If only one team does it, it's cheating. It's a man's game—no crying, no whining. Of course, life is not fair. Who said it ever was? Fairness is an ideal that people adhere to when they have no other resource to get what they want. When reason is no longer an option, coercion or acceptance are the other choices. Baseball is as close to fair as it gets. It's not perfect, but the rules keep the game played by very motivated and talented young men and women. The baseball gods seem to even out the mistakes made, much like karma does in life. How those situations are handled on the field is a reflection of lessons learned in life, and the resulting behavior is left to guide us closer and closer to a completely balanced life.

Chapter 17

2012 was one of the best years of baseball that I could remember. There were so many young players making a name for themselves. Nineteen- and twenty-year-olds were playing like seasoned veterans. There were also seasoned veterans playing like nineteen-year-olds. Derek Jeter and Chipper Jones had career years after fifteen years, at least in the big leagues. There were more teams in contention after 161 games, with division titles coming down to one game. There were two wildcard teams for the first time, with nine teams in each league in contention for a playoff spot in the last week of regular-season games. No, ho hum, here came the same old, same old again this year. Not for this sport. Baseball had taken hit after hit over recent years, in part due to steroids, and not only survived but was doing better than ever.

On the last day of the season, the Yankees were battling for the best record in the American League and the division lead. The Orioles, Athletics, and Rangers were one game back, so a one-game playoff was possible. The Yankees had no idea where they'd be playing in two days, let alone in two weeks. They did lead the American League with ninety-five wins, but they got swept four games by the Tigers in the playoffs. Awe shucks. Oh, well, there was always next year. For the first time, there were many good teams doing unreal things, and I continued to see things that I had never seen before. The passion for the game was alive and well. There might be a triple-crown winner for the first time since 1963. Miguel Cabrera of the Tigers was poised to win that crown. It wasn't likely that anyone would catch him. The only stat in jeopardy was home runs, so Josh Hamilton would have to hit at least two without Cabrera hitting another. It turned out that Miguel Cabrera won the crown. It turned out that the Giants took it all in the World Series and beat Detroit in a four-game sweep. The best pitching defeated the best hitting. San Fran was riding a wave of glory like never before, and because of the pitching and teamwork, they were unstoppable.

2013 was an even better year than 2012, if you could believe it. New players, retiring players, competitive baseball, and ten teams were involved in the playoff picture in the last week in the American League alone. Mariano Rivera and Andy Petite pitched their last games with the Yankees. The ceremony at Yankee Stadium for Mariano was epic. He was the last player wearing number 42, Jackie Robinson's retired number, and Mrs. Jackie Robinson helped retire it once and for all. Todd Helton retired from the game as the Rockies's best player ever after seventeen years with the club. He was given a pony as a retirement gift from the team, which seemed pretty normal for someone in Colorado. Twelve players were suspended for steroid use, and A-Rod was the only player to fight it. Although all the other players cheated, they at least owned up to it. Cheating and lying, in my opinion, made A-Rod a bum, just like Barry Bonds. Hopefully, the game was being cleaned up. Some guys were so strong, it was hard to tell, and the cheaters were always getting ahead of the testing, so we'll see.

The Indians had a really good year. They hired Terry Francona as manager and picked up Nick Swisher and Jason Giambi as veterans to help out the young kids on the field and in the clubhouse. They got their butts kicked by Detroit and Boston, and it was ugly. By the all-star break, they were still in it. The rest of the year proved to be feast or famine. They won ten games in a row at the end of the season and won home field advantage for a one-game playoff with Tampa Bay. However, they were handed their heads by Tampa, and it was a one-game post-season for the hapless lads.

I believe that baseball is in good hands. There is great hope and promise, and the Lord knows great baseball yet to be played. Note from 2021: The Indians aren't the Indians anymore. Baseball is not in good hands, and they have destroyed the very game I have loved all my life with their stupid idiocrasy. Weak, money-loving fools!

Chapter 18

Demon number 1: Most of my adult life, I have battled the demon of revenge—getting even. I have always felt compelled to right a wrong, get even, not take any crap, send a signal not to mess with me, etc. Since Nam, the means of pursuing this action have stepped up a few notches. Deceit, trickery, and disinformation all work toward an advantage. It means survival if you can perform consistently. For the first time, I have fought the revenge factor after my third divorce. I lost most of what I have worked for in a very rude and aggressive manner right after I had my second back surgery in less than a year in 2010. After a year of legal battles, I gave it all up for my health and sanity rather than continue a futile war. My ex found my new email and tried to blackmail me. My computer got a Trojan horse virus within twenty-four hours. It was my fault for sending her to website school! It brought back all the emotions I felt—anger and all the thoughts of revenge I had decided to put away.

In my mind, I carry out a complete scenario via an ambush or surprise attack that allows me the opportunity to inflict great damage. That is the way to ward off your enemies, so I feel that, in some way, it must be done. The problem is, and thank God I thought it through, it's illegal and immoral. The price of revenge is too high, so the problem or challenge is learning how to cope with the thoughts of revenge, stay within the law, and get right with God. It is said that if you seek revenge, dig two graves, one for yourself. The exhilaration of getting revenge is huge. It takes away all the anger and stress. The desire to carry out these thoughts can be very strong. It takes a lot of energy to maintain the proper balance. My point here is not to focus on the negative thoughts but rather on the tremendous effort it takes to maintain balance. And balance is what it's all about—balance in all aspects of life—mind, body, and spirit; balance in daily routines of exercise, eating, resting, and playing; balance in thought and pushing the limits of expectations. It sounds like a contradiction, but it isn't.

Think about it: is being balanced striving for less than excellence? No, being balanced means exercising all aspects of life equally hard. In order to grow, one must go beyond the norm or the expectation of one's very best. Imagine people sitting around the fire, waiting for the hunters to come back with food so they could all eat. There were no electronics, no shelters, no cars, no bikes, no bras (ha ha), and no way to imagine a better life. Just the same existence from generation to generation. Because a few men and women pushed beyond the norm or what was expected to be their best, today we have all the luxuries these pursued ideas have provided.

Chapter 19

I turned seventy years old on October 7, 2020. This was the first time a number affected me on my birthday. It is now hard to imagine having a really long life from here, but I have always believed that I will live to be one hundred years old or more. It's not a wish; it's a fact! With that said, I didn't know what to expect on my birthday, but I hoped a few people would come out and celebrate it with me. The seventh being on a Wednesday, I figured the weekend before or after my birthday might work for a few people. I invited Blaine and Bobbie Fagel, my nephew and niece, hoping they could make it. Blaine traveled every week, and Bobbie suffered from childhood diabetes, so there were restrictions. They couldn't make the trip, but Blaine called, and Bobbie sent a gift. Dee had a surprise seventieth birthday party that January, which was given by Nikki, her youngest daughter. With the help of the rest of us, Dee got all the bells and whistles with pictures, a DJ, food, gifts, and many friends with non-stop dancing and prancing. It was a blast, and it showed how much everyone loves and cares about Dee.

I had learned long ago that the worst disappointments came from the most unreasonable expectations. If you hope to fly, you can jump off a cliff and give it a shot. I guarantee you major disappointment because man cannot fly! See my point? I tried to be reasonable about my expectations, so when I thought about my birthday, I didn't think it would be like Dee's. I did, however, want people to come out here and help me celebrate my seventy years of existence. Yeah, it won't look so big when I'm one hundred, but it did then.

It was a quiet day. It was sunny and warm, and summer was turning into fall. Dee didn't wish me a happy birthday until later that day; she forgot. Ally, my daughter, called, and we had a nice chat.

Dee's kids, five girls, all sent me a text wishing me a happy birthday. I did not hear from anyone else. I didn't get any cards, gifts, or visitors. In fact, Dee spent the weekend at Kim's, her oldest daughter. As I tried to put this all into perspective and not be upset or disappointed, I realized just how much I meant to everyone in my life…not much. Dee said to me just two months before that I treated her better than anyone else ever had. Kind of confusing, huh? It was hard not to struggle over this because it was somewhat contradictory. So what did this mean? If it was all about family, then I was not family. Dee's girls liked me, and we got along, but I was not family. I had felt like this my whole life. Good things were for other people, not me. I'd play by the rules; it didn't matter. I served my country in the war; it didn't matter. I got two college degrees; it didn't matter. I never disrespected my parents; it didn't matter. I tried hard to have a family and be part of a family my whole life; it didn't matter. Not for me. The Lord knows that I am nowhere near perfect, but I am a good, God-fearing Christian. I have asked to be forgiven for all my sins, and there are many. I ask for strength and wisdom every day.

Chapter 20

Meeting Rich Davies in his hometown of Skokie, Illinois, was quite an experience. I knew him briefly from my vacation in Miami, but what I learned in a short period of time allowed me to know him better than anyone I had ever known. I met all of his friends, and they all felt the same way about him. They admired him, trusted him, and loved him. He had no air about him, nor was he arrogant or above anyone. He knew the truth about so many things that had either happened or were about to happen. His family felt the same way about him. He told his sister the day before her next birthday that if she went out to celebrate, it would be the last thing she ever did. She did not leave the house. Not on that birthday or any other birthday that I knew of.

We stayed busy doing something every day while I was there with all of his friends. One girl, let's call her Angie Cohen, had a rich daddy who gave her a GTO for the weekdays and a GTO for the weekends. She came and picked up Rich and me one day, and she took us to her daddy's very rich golf club. I had never seen money like this, but I had met more than one Jewish father, coming from a high school that was 90 percent Jewish. They were all the same... they hated me. I never had bad intentions with any of the girls I liked, and it was the same with Angie. We were a group of friends who spent time together, planning our adult years. Rich had the idea that we should all apply to Santa Monica Junior College and start our adult lives there, getting an education. I had college paid for per my parents' divorce agreement, as long as I went right after high school. It was still the summer of 1968, so the choice was mine. Four of us were accepted, and we were going to conquer the world. I was so excited that I could burst with joy. My life was finally changing for the better, and with friends I had wanted my whole life.

We were sitting around one day, and Rich proclaimed, "We're all going to California together!" I should have been jumping up and down, but I wasn't. Rich looked at me and asked, "We're going to California together, right?"

I said, "No." I knew that Rich knew what I meant, and it felt like I was crushing him.

"Why?" he asked.

"I can't go, Rich. I have to go to Vietnam."

"No, you don't, Ken. You're coming with us!"

"Rich, I'm not smart like you, but I know this the way you know things, and if I don't go now, I'll never make it home!" I don't know how I knew that. There were no voices talking to me, but I just knew.

Chapter 21

As Rich and his friends prepared for Santa Monica, I returned to Cleveland and prepared for Vietnam. There was no draft at that time, so I volunteered for the draft, which allowed me to serve two years instead of three had I enlisted. I left for the army and went to Fort Campbell, Kentucky, on January 27, 1969. I kept in touch with Angie so she could keep me in touch with Rich. I never got a letter back, in spite of writing every week. I graduated boot camp and got shipped to Fort Polk, Louisiana, nicknamed "Little Nam." We all thought that with boot camp over, this assignment would be more like a day job. Wow! We were wrong! We arrived at "Little Nam' about 2:30 a.m., and our drill sergeant jumped on the bus and just started ripping us a new one. "Ladies, while you are here, you will NOT walk anywhere. You will double-time. If you are not in a chow line, you will be doing double time, or I will drop you and you'll push out twenty." We were stunned to say the least, and we trained, trained, and trained some more until we dropped. We were taught how to fight and how to use weaponry, explosives, and military tactics. We became the number 1 platoon in our brigade in all training areas. I remembered asking "Top" why he was so hard on us, and he said, "Son, I've spent two years in Nam watching good young men like you die, so I came back here to train you right so that wouldn't keep happening!" Yeah, I was speechless. I was also honored to have been trained by a man like him.

There were still no return letters from Angie. Nothing from Rich, either. On my way home on leave, I stopped at Chicago O'Hare Airport and called Angie. She said she had not received one letter. I confirmed that she had given me the right address and assured her she'd get my new address as soon as I got stationed in Nam. Well, I was sure glad I got that straight. I couldn't wait to hear from Rich. I started writing to Angie as soon as I was assigned an APO address. I was now in the 101st Airborne Army Ranger L Co. unit. Two weeks later, all my mail to Angie was returned to me, "address unknown."

Chapter 22

This story was about my last month in the country—where I was, who I was with, and what happened. It was just another day in Nam, and I had learned a lot in L Co. Rangers with the 101st Airborne. I was the old guy now, and it was my turn to teach our young guys how to survive and get home safely. I wasn't young anymore, and the war and death had aged me. I was strictly into survival. Having gone from L Co. LRRP's to the 2/327 "No Slack" battalion, I was considered a veteran leader.

The recon platoon had a lot of cherries in it (new guys). We were strictly recon made up of two teams, six men each. We did a lot of work around the Fire Base Rifle and Tomahawk. Both fire bases were west of Phu Loc village. There was a great deal of activity there, but we could rarely engage with it. It seemed like we were always one step behind the VC, and Charlie just didn't want to fight.

It was early May 1970. Our two teams were standing down, just west of Phu Loc, in an abandoned school house. It was just the shell of a concrete building with no doors or windows. We were in between the village and the foothills, so we could monitor incoming activities. They just assigned a "shake and bake" staff sergeant to lead our two teams because our previous team leader, Mo, had finished his tour of duty and was headed home. A "shake and bake" is trained in the States and doesn't know squat about what's going on or how to lead men. Mo was a good man and a fine leader who had kept most of his men alive. Now it was up to Spock and me to do the same. Spock was the other team leader and had been there as long as me. We were both combat-tested, so it was our job to teach all the new guys. Sergeant Shake and Bake was a real cherry himself and, unfortunately, had the attitude and misconception that he knew everything, which made him very dangerous. He was the guy who got everybody killed but himself. He had no intention of listening to Spock or me. He thought he was just so smart! He tried to lay down the law with us and proclaimed, "If I ever catch you sleeping on guard duty, I will kill you." Yeah, what the hell did he know about killing a man or war? Spock and I had a good laugh, but we knew we'd better find out what kind of men we had before it was too late. Little did we know it already was.

The VC would use a number of different trails to come down the mountains into the village at night for supplies. Spock and I decided to set up an L-shaped ambush on one of the trails that night, and at exactly 2300 hours, we'd light up the trail and pull off a fake firefight. Everyone would think it was real, and we could gauge their responses accordingly. We knew there were only two kinds of people: those who react and those who don't, and you would never know who's who until tested. I told Spock that we'd know what kind of men we had by 2305 hours. At 2300, we lit up the trail with red and yellow smoke grenades and fired every weapon we had, like it was the fourth of July. The luminescent flares lit up the night, and we were on full rock and roll. Everybody responded the right way, and we were really proud of them and relieved. I had Shake and Bake on my team, so as I set the guard rotation, I put him on at 0400 to 0500 hours. That's 4:00 a.m. to 5:00 a.m. for you, college boys! The guards were set, and the AO was secure. The firefight might have been staged, but we might have given away our position too, so we had to be vigilant. This wasn't over yet. I couldn't forget the threat leveled at us, and I didn't want any unnecessary BS being dumped on our men.

I grabbed a little shut-eye so I could keep an eye on everyone throughout the night, and Spock did the same. A little before 0500, I felt a tap on my shoulder; it was Spock. I locked and loaded on him until I saw who it was and then lowered my AR. He pointed at Shake and Bake, lying there sound asleep on guard duty! I stuck my AR up his nose as Spock kicked him in the ribs good and hard, and I said, "By your own rules, you're dead. You sorry, son of a bitch." The weary-eyed little bastard lay there rubbing his eyes while we all surrounded his cowardly ass. Most of us were in disbelief, and

Spock and I dared not think about what would be next. We knew we had a real problem here and didn't quite know what to do about it. Everybody sensed the danger that lurked within Shake and Bake, and they were looking at us to fix it. We all had to be on the same page, or we would be in really serious trouble.

Chapter 23

The teams spent a few more days at the abandoned school house. During the day, we'd play a knife-throwing game called "eat the peg." It honed our knife-throwing skills, and it was also healthy competition. It built teamwork and morale while passing away the daytime hours when we weren't on a mission. The object of the game was to stick the knife in the ground by flipping it off various body parts in sequence. It began by flipping it off the right pinky finger and doing all the digits, then the wrist, elbow, shoulder, head, and then back down the left side of the body in opposite order. The first one to finish won. The last one to finish lost. With five players, the first winner would pound a three- or four-inch wooden peg into the dirt four times, the next winner three times, the next two times, and then the next one time. The loser had to pull the peg out of the ground with his teeth and his hands behind his back. This was a game I NEVER lost. It was bad enough that I was in Vietnam. I sure wasn't going to eat their dirt.

My team consisted of five men—Gadagni, Sugarbear, Rat, Blondie, and Tran. Gadagni was a pudgy Italian from New York City. Brooklyn, I believe. He was rough around the edges, but he was always there when you needed him. He loved a mad minute as much as anyone. A mad minute was used to test weapons and expend ammo that might have been compromised by the heat or humidity. Who doesn't love a mad minute? Sugarbear was a small, good-looking Black man, wise beyond his years. He'd had a rough life growing up in Chicago, but he seemed to appreciate it. At least he never complained. Rat was a tall, thin young man from West Virginia. He had a cocky but confident attitude and was very reliable. He never talked much about his life or future, but I could tell that he was troubled.

Blondie was a young, seventeen-year-old baby face. He joined the army to gain the respect of his father. He was never treated well at home. He was probably abused, and he thought maybe one day he could prove himself here. Tran was a South Vietnamese Kit Carson scout who worked with us because of his knowledge of the area. He knew where the enemy was, but mostly he knew where they weren't.

Orders came down for a base camp stand-down and rappelling training for the new guys. I was very proficient at rappelling, so the teaching job was mine. If you have never rappelled before, it's like jumping off a cliff with a safe landing. It is very cool. I liked rappelling out of a chopper better than off a tower, but we trained off the tower. Spock and I both hoped the downtime would help us figure out how to deal with "sleepy." Since we'd been in the field for over a month, a hot shower and a meal sounded pretty good.

Chapter 24

While doing a one-year tour, everyone got to go on an R&R (rest and recuperation) for a week. We could go to Bangkok; Hong Kong; Sydney, Australia; or Hawaii. Spock and I had been in the country for over ten months without an R&R, so we went to Sydney for a week. Spock left three days before me, and I finished the rappelling training. We would meet in Sydney then. Spock was going to check out the hot spots, find a couple hotties to play with, and basically pave the way for a good time away from hell. There was no problem there because we were both confident as hell and couldn't wait.

I arrived at Sydney Airport three days later, as planned. I was greeted by Sgt. Roberts, an engineer from our unit who went to Sydney with Spock. I didn't think much of Spock not meeting me at the airport because I was sure he was keeping the hotties warm for us. Sgt. Roberts told me that something was wrong, and I had to go with him. I asked what was wrong. "I'm not sure," he said. "Everything was fine until last night, when Spock said he didn't feel well. Within a short period of time, he said he felt really bad and wanted to go to the hospital, so I got a cab and took him right away."

"Is he still there?" I asked.

"That's where we're going now."

I knew something was really wrong, and I wasn't being told everything. Roberts knew Spock and I were really close, so I told him to tell me what the hell was going on and stop beating around the bush!

"Spock died last night." I couldn't comprehend what I just heard. We were there to party. A hiatus from death. What kind of cruel joke could this be? Nobody would play a practical joke like this. Everybody knows I hate practical jokes. They aren't practical at all.

I didn't remember the ride to the hospital. We didn't speak again for some time. When we got to the hospital, I was taken to the attending nurse. I asked to see the attending doctor. She refused because I wasn't family. I asked what he died from, and I was denied the information. I wasn't family. I told the nurse that I was as close to him as it got and demanded to be told. The nurse said, "All I can tell you is that he had some kind of sleeping sickness virus, and it was never diagnosed or treated." Spock did look pretty worn out, but who wouldn't after ten months of combat? I asked for his parents contact information so I could tell them what a brave man their son was. I was denied again! I didn't take no for an answer very well, let alone three times. I grabbed the nurse by the throat, slammed her into the wall, and told her that if she didn't tell me, I'd give her a sleeping sickness virus. The next thing I knew, I was being thrown out on my ass by two very big dudes. They said that if I ever came back, they'd have me arrested. My parting comment was, "Only if I let you see me."

Chapter 25

The next few days were a blur for me. I got a room at Alice's Motel, and Sgt. Roberts kept his distance—not out of fear, but out of respect. Having time to mourn the loss of anyone was not a luxury afforded in Vietnam, let alone my best buddy. I eventually went out to a couple of parties and took in the sights. I mostly hung out at the beach, where I felt most at home, but I just couldn't shake what happened. This was not how it was supposed to be. I was finally in the company of round eyes, and I could have cared less. I was no longer optimistic.

Roberts and I went back to Nam together, and we took our sweet-ass time. Life was really messing with my mind, and I wanted control back. From here on out, I was making the rules. I met a chopper pilot in Da Nang, and he offered to take me for a ride in his Loach, a light observation helicopter. It was a pretty hairy scout flight. I was all in. It's amazing how much respect a Ranger gets from other soldiers. Officers would salute us, and nobody gave us any crap. This pilot was buzzing the treetops like a hedge trimmer, giving me the thrill of a lifetime. I asked if he'd ever been shot down. He said, "No, I come up on Charlie so low and fast, he can't hit the broad side of a barn." I asked how often he drew fire. He said, "Everyday, hell, that's my job." Two minutes didn't go by, and we were drawing fire like the fourth of July. I spoke too soon. I thought it would be a real lick to get shot down right after R&R and being AWOL to boot. The pilot was right, though. He was so fast and so low that Charlie couldn't hit the broad side of a barn!

Roberts and I got back to Camp Eagle the next day to resume what was left of our tour of duty. I was getting short because I only had a month to go. The flight back was beautiful, and it reminded me of how pristine the country could be if only there wasn't a war going on. That was how I felt when I first came here. This country was so beautiful. The ocean was incredible. Further inland were the rice paddies. Beyond that lay the villages that sat at the bottom of the mountains, which sprawled out as far as the eye could see.

Chapter 26

I walked back into my company compound at the "no slack" battalion and headed toward the hooch, where we bunked as teammates. I assumed they already knew about Spock's death. The bunks were empty—no personal belongings, no tape players for music, and nobody there. That seemed pretty odd because if they were in the field, their belongings would still be there. I was then approached by a spec 4 I didn't know. "Are you Fagel?

"Yeah, who wants to know?" I had a really uneasy feeling about this. He should have been with the team if they were in the field. He said that he had some bad news, and then I knew.

"Your teams were walked into an ambush, and they were all killed except for Shake and Bake. I was stunned. How could this be? Why was I being told this by a stranger and not my CO? Why was everyone killed except Shake and Bake? I knew this guy was going to get people killed, but this? I was told by HQ to go back to the field with sleepy, and I flatly refused. They didn't know what to do, so they sent me to the battalion commander, Col. Pickett. This guy was sitting in an air-conditioned office behind this huge cherry desk in his starched fatigues and spit-shined boots, and he told me to stand at attention while he dressed me down.

"Who the hell do you think you are disobeying a direct order?"

I replied, "I'm not going to the field with Shake and Bake, and that's final." He asked if I was some kind of coward. I went slack and told him, "If you think I'm some kind of coward, then why don't you go to the field with me, and we'll see who comes back!" He was flabbergasted. Nobody had ever spoken to him like that before. He got all my men killed. He was protecting the guy who did it, and he was calling me a coward! "You just try to kill me, you rotten bastard." I should have been busted right there and put in the brig, but I wasn't. He wouldn't go to the field with me either. I figured by his behavior and not busting me that he was really afraid of something. But what? He was covering for Shake and Bake, so who was his daddy? I went and found sleepy up at the chow hall and asked him what happened, and he wouldn't tell me. I told him that the next time I saw him, I'd kill him. Spock is dead. Both teams are dead. No one would talk to me. And apparently, I could say whatever I wanted with zero consequences.

I got shipped to an FOB (forward observation base), just south of Phu Loc. The AO was about fifty square meters. There were a few GIs and several ARVN (South Vietnamese Army) posted there with a radio bunker. This compound basically relayed communication between the fire bases and Camp Eagle. Smaller posts like that also called it "radio relay."

Chapter 27

I was now under the command of MSgt. Bowen. Top was a hard-core lifer, and he took a shine to me. He told me that he understood what I was going through and that he had my back. Hmmmmm, very interesting. Top kept me busy taking the supply truck to fire bases Rifle and Tomahawk and dumping the garbage at the dump, down by the ocean. Since I was already there, I'd spend a few hours swimming and chilling out after I was done at the dump. This was technically AWOL, but I didn't care. What are they gonna do? Send me to Nam and kill all my teammates? I was on top of my game. I was in charge. I was confident again. Now I had two days to go, and I was the enemy they couldn't kill in my mind. I was so short that I needed a ladder to see the top of a claymore.

Top came to me late that afternoon. He didn't know that I'd been at the beach, and I wasn't going to tell him. I had tried that back home with my brothers when we all skipped school, and it was harder to pull off then. I was still not sure we did.

"Fagel, I don't want you sleeping on top of the bunker tonight." I always slept there so I could see, hear, and smell what was coming.

"Yeah, yeah," I said.

"Fagel, I'm not fucking around with you now, son. No sleeping on the bunker tonight." That was very out of character for Top, and I wondered what was going on. I told him that if he didn't want me in the bunker, he could put me on guard duty.

"Fine, 0100 hours at the radio bunker." What the heck did he know that I didn't? Maybe I was about to find out.

I took my post at 0100 hours, which was a foxhole just outside the radio bunker. It faced QL1, or highway 1, and it was one hundred yards from Phu Loc. The shit hit the fan at 0130 hours. Mortars peppered the compound with regularity for a couple of hours. Then we were hit with a frontal assault from QL1. "Gooks in the wire! Gooks in the wire!" I screamed. As I looked around briefly, I saw that all the ARVNs had deserted their posts and left the weapons behind. The radiomen were in the bunker, huddled in the corner, and screaming for help. I was all alone, and I refused to die. After all, I was optimistic and confident as hell. I lit up the perimeter with every weapon at my disposal. Popping flares to keep the perimeter lit up, I was dropping every gook who tried getting into the compound. I would go from using an AR15 to an M60 machine gun, an M79 grenade launcher, hand grenades, and claymore mines to cover every inch of ground. I fanned my fire from left to right and in and out all the way to QL1. They had to get up a sloped embankment to get into the perimeter, so I continued firing everything I had over and over and over again, like a record stuck in a groove. When I thought I was about to lose it all, I cried out to God and my mother. It all stopped. It was about 0730 hours.

Chapter 28

The smoke was heavy, and the compound was in near-complete destruction. I crawled out of the foxhole and started walking around what was left. There were only two of us and an enemy body count of thirty-two. Where was Top? Where were the two radio men? It was just me and the other soldier who came from the other side of the compound. This was some kind of bad dream, and I didn't know how I survived it. I had called out to God and my mother. I knew God heard me because he saved me from this onslaught. I knew my mother heard me because she said she thought she heard me at that very moment when she was at work. She walked from her office to the lobby and asked the ladies there where I was. They said, "Oh, Eileen, Ken is in Vietnam."

The morning was not as bright and luminous as usual. The ground was covered in blood, and the sky was a gloomy gray. Jeeps were overturned, the ground was pocked like the moon, and the smell of gun powder was everywhere. The most devastating site was the bunker I used to sleep on. It took a direct hit and was completely destroyed. The gravity of this didn't hit me right away, but it would. The bunker had taken the worst of it. *Don't sleep on that damn bunker tonight, Fagel.* I kept hearing it over and over again. My mind was spinning, and as I looked at all the dead bodies, I asked myself if I had done all this. No one else was there. How could I have done all this? No one else was there. At what price? Freedom?

A 2 1/2-ton truck came down QL1, full of new guys. They were all taking pictures of the dead bodies, and I was repulsed. I jumped into the truck and screamed at them to stop. "Do you think this is the glory of war? Do you think this is going to get you through this whole mess? Well, you are wrong. Do you hear me? You are wrong!"

As I walked back into the compound, a helicopter landed across QL1. Col. Pickett got out of it and had a silver star pinned to his chest for what would be called the most formidable defensive effort by the 101st in the Vietnam War. How could that be? He wasn't even there. The men were left out of it. Both of them. Where was Top? How did he know what was about to happen? Why was my bunker the most devastated? Why did Top warn me? He said he'd have my back. There were two days to go. In three days, all my dreams and hopes would become a reality. There were two days to go. I couldn't think like that. I'd become dangerous.

I went back to Camp Eagle and walked into the company area, and no one would talk to me. They were all a bunch of pissants anyway. Who cared! The CO busted me, so he could get his pound of flesh. What a coward! They couldn't kill me, so I'd won in my eyes. Nobody could face me or live up to what I had become, let alone get in my face. Nobody understood the gravity of the situation. Nobody cared. I thought we were all on the same side. Boy, was I wrong! The truth of the matter was that I was the last man standing. That new shake and bake got all my men killed. When I returned from Sydney, I was a loose end. When I refused to go back to the field with him, they had to come up with plan B. That might be why I wasn't busted for insubordination. They had other plans. I could talk if I was in the brig. I couldn't say a word if I was dead. The plan failed, if that's what it was. Now they were scared, and they knew I was out there somewhere. They should be because I was the enemy they couldn't kill.

Chapter 29

Another year had gone by. It was 2021, and our country had gone to hell. Dee had throat cancer, and everything had changed. I turned seventy-one, and I lowered my expectations about a birthday party. I wasn't disappointed. With Dee being so sick, I could hardly make this about me. Daily routines and habits all changed. Doctor appointments, testing, more doctor appointments, and all that entailed changed everything. Her daughters were there for her, as always. I admired that. I could have been jealous, but I wasn't. That would be weak and petty. I changed my habits for her sake and promised to do whatever I could to help every day. We had to fight to get her welfare, Medicare, and the treatment she needed, and we found out just how broken the system was. Health care being yet another big business, you'd think we could get excellent treatment, but I guess the society of corrupt politicians wouldn't line their pockets the way they do, in my humble opinion.

I wanted to speak about Dee's illness and tell the story as I saw it. She got sick in the fall of 2021, and she was seeing a number of doctors and getting tested when a lump in her throat was found. The doctor was supposed to do a biopsy, test the lump, and then proceed with the right treatment. The doctor tried to remove or debride the tumor, but for some reasons, it made the situation ten times worse. The hospital administration held up any further treatment because her Medicare wasn't approved yet. The cancer got exponentially worse, so I contacted our congressman, David Joyce, for help. He got Dee full coverage, and it was retroactive from the time of the first visit. We were thrilled, to say the least. However, the cancer had advanced so much by that time that they recommended a laryngectomy—the removal of the larynx. They took so much tissue from her throat that they needed two donor sites to replace and rebuild what was removed. One site was her left forearm, and the other was her left thigh. The surgery was awful, and the girls made sure that I didn't see her like that right away.

Dee came home after her stay in the hospital, and we all had to learn how to care for her on a daily basis, and it was quite involved. Kim is a nurse, so she led the way. I'm no dummy, but I didn't know how to do any of this, so I learned from her. She was able to stay for a couple of months. God bless her! Donna, Jenny, and Haley came on off-hours to learn the whole system of her healthcare. Dee needed to start the chemo and radiation for five days a week over about a six-week period in Mentor, so she stayed with Nikki in Painesville for a couple of months. Nikki took care of her and provided her healthcare around the clock. Jenny and Mandy helped and visited as much as they could, as well as Haley. Donna took care of the business end, and Nikki took care of ordering all the supplies needed and her immediate needs. In the months that Dee had been home, she had improved steadily and become cancer-free. In that time, we celebrated Christmas out here in Williamsfield, as well as a wel-come-home party and then a surprise birthday party on January 21, 2022—a day before Dee's birthday. Haley made the most beautiful video of family and friends individually saying a few words to Dee about her strength and recovery. Everyone had beautiful things to say to Mom, Nana, Dee, Doll, and Sis. To see a family come together like that in the worst of times, with nothing but support and positive thoughts, was a blessing. To see this family come together to cele-brate Dee's survival was a gift.

By 2023, in March, Dee had been cancer-free for a few months. She had been gaining her weight back and healing in every respect. She still had ways to go, but we had met some pretty incredible peo-ple, and I could honestly say that this whole experience had humbled me. In all of my experiences, I could honestly say that I believe cour-age is acting in spite of fear and believing you will win.

Chapter 30

When I first arrived in Vietnam and got to my new unit, I had one goal: to make it home in one piece without injury in 366 days. Our tour of duty was one year. It was a double-edged sword because there were two contrasting outcomes. Knowing how long you must survive in order to go home meant there was a light at the end of the tunnel. That's the upside. Getting close to your ETS (estimated time of separation) made men very dangerous. They started to think past the moment. In a way, it was a very Zen type of mentality needed to survive. Think only of the now, the moment, and the very present that you were in. When you practice something repeatedly, you perform on muscle memory; you don't take time to think; you just do it. Subsequently, when you stop to think, you become very dangerous.

I had a dream about what I'd do when I got home; everyone did. It was how you got through the day and night. The thought got little actual attention. The comfort was in knowing that you had a plan. It was easier to stay in the moment if you could put that part of the future aside, knowing it was safe there.

"Hey troop," said one of the Rangers in the unit I just volunteered for. "You married?"

"No," I said.

"Got a girl?"

"Yeah." He said I wouldn't for long. No one escaped "Dear John." He had just gotten a "Dear John" letter from his wife. He still had six months to go.

I dreamed I would kiss the soil on the ground when I returned home. I dreamed my family would meet me with open arms and be full of joy. I dreamed of seeing my closest friends and telling them all about it. The Lord knew that I'd need help working through it all, but how could they ever know? I dreamed I had a job of respect I earned from surviving one year as a Ranger. I got so much respect there that I knew life had finally changed for me. I earned it, and I was super proud.

When day 366 finally came, I began to think of going home. I got to the processing station in Camp Eagle that morning in spite of a major attack in Phu Loc two nights before. I got the last seat on the departing flight. Looking back, it was funny, but not so much at the time. We boarded the plane from the front and rear. Everyone filled the seats in front of me, which resulted in all seats being taken. I stood there in disbelief, then walked to the front and took an empty seat. The stewardess promptly said that it was her seat, and I told her that I wasn't getting off, so she damn well better find me another seat. Lucky for me, I got a seat at the back with the prisoners. A poor kid went home in cuffs for smoking weed. Tokyo came and went, and the next stop was Anchorage, Alaska. We were due to arrive at 0230 hours. It was June, so it was light all night. We landed on time, and I was primed to kiss the ground of my homeland. We filled off the plane for resupplies and cleaning, so we had a nice terminal to stretch our legs in. Before I had another thought, we were attacked by several young people who were protesting the war. This was the first time I was unarmed in a year. This was my country. These were Americans. What the hell just happened? Too bad for them. The first thing we learned in the army was hand-to-hand combat. It was not something you forgot. We were shuffled back onto the plane, and no one said a word.

Chapter 31

I finally got to Cleveland, and when my mother first saw me, she said, "You look half dead!" My family looked at me like I was a freak. Not one person said a word.

I saw my friends that night, both Nam vets, and said, "I finally get to tell you guys what just happened to me, what I survived."

They said, "Screw that. We don't want to hear it." I was stunned, to say the least. This moment of return that I dreamed about was only in my mind. What was I returning to? Why was there so much hatred, and why was it aimed at me? The whole country changed, and the rules were thrown out with the morals. The protesting was shameful, and the conduct of our government was worse. Ah, the good old days were gone. That was back when we had freedom of speech. No one dared yell "fire" in a crowd because it was irresponsible. Now it was considered to be pushing the limits. Nope, still irresponsible.

Changing the meaning of words does not change anything, other than an open admission of ignorance. Gay used to mean happy. Who doesn't want to be happy? Bad used to be bad; now it means good. Fag used to mean cigarette; now it means queer. Dope used to mean drugs; now it means cool. Do you know that, by rule, lazy people work harder at being lazy than they do at being productive? Why don't people just learn the language? Get a Webster's and look up every word you can't define as soon as you see or hear it. And by the way, # is pound; it's not a name. The point is simple; call it what it is.

So what does one do when just about everything he believes in is not real? (Future hint: Get a Bible.) There is no respect, honor, bravery, courage, or character that anyone ever sees in me. I was anything but these, and all this came from people who knew nothing. They weren't there. At best, they heard stories so blown out of proportion that one had to ask if they were written by Oliver Stone. Nam vet himself, and yet he perpetuated lies about that war. Do you really think soldiers walked around aimlessly murdering villagers with no chain of command or authority to act under? Have you looked into the population of Leavenworth, where soldiers who commit war crimes go?

Chapter 32

After a year of travel, living in Waikiki Beach for six months, and hitchhiking across the country, I settled in Orlando, Florida, with my brother and started what would be eight years of college and a variety of jobs in veterinary clinics and college labs. My goal was to become a veterinarian. My first task was learning how to spell it. I ultimately earned a BS in biology and a BA in psychology. Thank God for my Webster's! I was engrossed in all I did, and I drowned out Vietnam for twelve years. Then I crashed big time. That was when I met Dr. Knake.

I learned that there was no going home. My dreams were not attainable in the real world. My dream of being at home with family and friends was not realistic. Kissing the ground, I was once able to walk on didn't mean anything anymore. My family was shocked to see me this way. I was weighing 130 pounds with gaunt, sunken eyes, blackened by trauma. My friends were afraid to talk to me or ask me what it was like or how I was doing. The people I ran into looked at me like I was crazy and whispered behind my back. My language was shocking. No one ever asked me about my experience in Nam, and when one dumbass did, the question was, "How many people did you kill?" Advice to all: Don't ever ask a soldier that question. If you want to know what a man has gone through, ask him about his experience there. Break the ice with the oldest question alive: "How was the weather there? Is it true that, in heat, it's better to go commando (no undies)?" If you said that to me, I'd probably talk to you. A friend looks for ways to be a true friend. That's what a veteran needs the most. I couldn't make sense of all the violence, contradictions, and politics. I heard one thing and saw another. "We're not going to Cambodia or Laos." But we did. A friend to talk to who will listen to try to help make sense of this puzzle, and most of all, how to adapt back into civilian life and drop all the survival tactics that don't apply here—or do they? Note to self: Are survival tactics necessary in civilian life? Answer to self: Duh!

Chapter 33

I no longer believe that this is a free country or that we have the rights the constitution says we do. We are all slaves to the wealthy and privileged—also known as demons or slaves to the devil. I have been paying that price since Nam, when I dared to open my mouth about the hypocrisy and injustice going on there. War is big business. War in a country that borders on the largest opium fields in the world is also big business. Do you think it's a coincidence that there is an opium epidemic in this country? The French occupied Vietnam until they got their ass kicked in WWII. They reoccupied Vietnam around 1946 after the war, and then the US occupied it. Rather than help Ho Chi Minh reunify the country, we took the side of South Vietnam and went to war.

Kennedy was the first president to send troops there, but he had reservations. After his assassination, Johnson escalated the war big time. His presidency was a failure, so he chose not to run for a second term. Then we got Nixon. What a bum! Billboards were made asking if we would buy a used car from this guy! Nobody believed him, and yet he was elected. He swore we were not in Laos. That was a lie. Our unit went there often. Since we knew how to read a map, we knew exactly where we were. The black market was a huge business there on both sides. Supplies were stolen off the train headed north from Saigon by the Vietnamese and sold back to the US soldiers and anyone else with money. As a Ranger, I moved around a lot to many different places and got to see much more than most. What we saw made me wonder if this was why we were so vilified in our own country. I saw a movie called *Air America* that starred Mel Gibson, Robert Downy Jr., and Nancy Travis in 1990. The plot of the film was based on a nonfiction book chronicling the CIA-financed airline used to transport weapons and supplies in Cambodia, Laos, and Vietnam during the Vietnam War. I had always wondered if it wasn't much more than that. We were lied to about everything concerning Vietnam, so I had to wonder what was really being transported that required a "civilian" airline to do it. I suppose we'll never really know.

After 9/11, we started a war in Afghanistan. We spent twenty years fighting there and were left in disgrace, leaving behind all the instruments of war and destruction. Located there is the second-largest opium field in the world. The efforts in Vietnam and Afghanistan were never to win a war. All the lives taken and destroyed on both sides for what? Records show that over eight hundred thousand lives have been lost from drug-related overdoses.

Chapter 34

When I arrived in Vietnam, we had five days of P training. It prepared us for the weather, the enemy, and our responsibilities. On day five, we were visited by an army Ranger whose job it was to recruit for their unit. I never went to jump school, and I did not go to Ranger school because I was only a two-year draftee. Ron "mother" Rucker was as strac a soldier as I'd ever seen—black beret, camouflaged fatigues only worn by Rangers, and spit-shined boots. "Gentlemen, do you want to hump through these boonies with twenty smoking, toking, joking, screaming idiots getting your balls blown off, or do you want to go out for five days and back in for five days with five highly trained Rangers to gather intel with the full support of the entire military force at our disposal?"

Well, I was told never to volunteer for anything or to open my mouth while in Vietnam. "I'm in, mother. Where do I sign?" I knew this was right, just like I knew when I had to go.

I was sent up north to Camp Eagle, home of the 101st Airborne, L Co. Ranger unit. We were given a week to get acclimated before we were assigned to a team. I was testing my AR15 in a firing pit, and the noise was so loud that I went deaf in one ear. I was examined and told that it would be temporary, so I wasn't assigned to a team yet. Everybody busted my chops by pretending to say something to me, and I tried like heck to understand them. The joke was on me. I was surrounded by mimes acting out a comedy routine. Normally, I'd have been pretty ticked off, but I realized that these hard-core Rangers had a sense of humor. That was good. All they'd seen and been through didn't dampen their spirits. Of course, I hadn't met everyone yet because there were a few guys who were very troubled and damaged. They extended their tour there because they couldn't stand being home or around anyone who "didn't get it." They were all good men, but they had been through hell and back. I knew I had to watch, listen, learn, and keep my mouth shut. My hearing came back the following week, and I was assigned to a team.

We always had a pre-mission overflight to assess the surroundings of our AO (area of operation). We'd cover four grid squares on the map and pick out a number of insertion and extraction points. You never know, so be prepared. These multifaceted plans left little room for failure. The overflight was successful, so our mission was set for the next day. Our job was to be quiet, smooth, and undetectable. We carried about one hundred pounds in our rucksacks and taped down everything that could make noise. I had questions galore, but my biggest question was this: Our AR's would fire eighteen rounds in 1.2 seconds. Well, then what? My team leader showed me how to tape two magazines together so I could switch them out without hunting for the next one. It was a great idea. It didn't take long to see how well that worked because we made contact the first day. When the firefight was over, I realized that I had never stopped firing back. Where the heck were my magazines? I looked behind me, and there they were. I changed magazines so fast that I never gave it a thought. I realized just how good these men were at fighting and surviving, and I knew that if I followed their lead, I would get that good too.

Chapter 35

Our next mission was an odd one because our LZ (landing zone) was a plateau surrounded by mountain ridges. The *Art of War* says, "Never fight uphill." Okay, so we had that covered. Our insertion was hot. We were taking fire from all sides. Our AO was the Ashau Valley, and that's where Hamburger Hill is. Our unit was there in May '69. It was now July '69. Once we were inserted, we realized that the vegetation was so thick that we couldn't get off the plateau. We were stuck. The chopper couldn't land, so we were ordered to stay put until the next day. I was the only new guy on the team, so I watched, listened, and learned—sign language, no talking. The enemy was trying to find us with mortars, and our job was to stay hidden and quiet.

We set up our NDP (night defensive position) and dug in for the long haul. My job was to guard from 0400 to 0500 hours and not make a sound. We had our dehydrated LRRP rations and water, and we dug in for the night. I was ready for my watch and kept my ears open because we couldn't see a thing. Mortars were blowing up all around us, but luckily Charlie's aim sucked. About ten minutes into my watch, I heard movements about two feet from me. I was afraid the enemy could hear my heart, so I stopped breathing. I was scared. It seemed to last for an eternity, but finally my watch ended, and my team leader took over. I signaled to him the movement I was hearing, and he gave me a thumbs-up. I didn't get back to sleep because I was ready to rock and roll. I was not going to be captured. I remembered that game back home, and I learned my lesson.

It was now daylight, and the rest of the team looked pretty calm. Damn, these guys are good! Everybody started patting me on the back and giving me a thumbs-up. I had no idea why. It turned out that the movement I heard was a rat getting after my empty LRRP ration. I thought it was the enemy, and because I never gave up our position, it showed my team that I was cool under pressure. I still smile when I think about that. I'd been trying to make a good impression my entire life, and it always seemed to fail. When I finally succeeded, it was with the toughest men in the army. That's right, I'm gonna be a badass. Hoowaa! That's Ranger badass!

My next mission was a doozy, and it was about a week later than the last one. We were inserted in tall elephant grass, so we had to jump out of the chopper about ten feet. The pilot turned to me and said, "You guys are nuts for jumping out." I told him that he was nuts for not jumping because they were shooting at them! The chopper continued to take fire as we scrambled into the brush, and then there was an eerie calm that fell over the jungle. The chopper was out of range. The shooting stopped, and we moved through the jungle like ballet dancers on stage. The world stage of war was a ballet in the sense that every move was choreographed, and all the parts moved in unison with the others. We were quiet, deliberate, and all on the same page, as if we were one moving part. How cool is that? We moved well into our AO and found a nice little spot to set up just under a nearby ridgeline. We made sure not to disturb any part of the area we were in, and we did not leave it any differently from the way we found it. We were ghosts, never there. Boo! We set up our NDP and took turns on our guard duty—six men in the jungle completely camouflaged, not making a sound all night long. Part of our NDP was putting out claymore mines as a defensive tactic.

Our psychological warfare included looking bigger and tougher than we were. Our Ar15s had shorter barrels with a wide flash, so one AR sounded like five. So five ARs sounded like twenty-five. We could call in all kinds of support, and we could call in the rockets to within fifty yards of our position. Military protocol was normally no closer than one hundred yards. Yes, we were that good. No one questioned us. The sun was rising, and our team leader signaled to us that we had an "unfriendly" sitting on top of one of our claymore mines. Claymores were filled with about a pound of C-4. These people were North Vietnamese in uniform, heavily armed, and in very large numbers. We couldn't retrieve the mine. We couldn't leave it there. Hmmmm, what would choice number 3 be? Blow the mine. Well, that gave us away. What was the downside? The enemy would know they had company. What was the upside? We could kill the guard and create absolute chaos. Well, it was one, two, or three. What were we fighting for? Yeah, Arlo Guthrie popped into my head. Go figure.

We blew the mine and ran like hell. We had several escape routes preplanned and a few extraction points as well. We zigged, zagged, and kept ahead of dozens, if not many, more North Vietnamese for what seemed like forever. We called in for an extraction point, and we just kept dancing our way through the jungle. The whole day seemed to fly by, and we were not going to be extracted at that point. We stopped just short of another ridgeline and set up our NDP. Extraction was set for the next morning, and we'd be yanked out with McGuire rigs because the chopper had no landing zone. That rig was basically three loops and a rope, taking three men at a time. The morning came, the choppers were on their way, and we were ready to go. I was with the first extraction, and as we were lifted out, we could see over that ridgeline and realized that there were a massive number of NVA just waiting for us. Had we moved any further the day before, we'd be goners. We started taking fire, so we unlocked our arms and swung out like a pendulum in order to make three targets instead of one. It worked, and the next thing you know, we were getting the ride of our lives. The rest of the team was extracted safely as well. When we landed, the chopper pilot told us that we were a bunch of crazy bastards, and he'd kill us if we ever did that again. Knowing me, I kept my mouth shut. Yeah, right! I told the man that he was one hell of a pilot, and he got us all back safe and sound.

The draft had just been enacted for Vietnam, and they picked based on birthdates. I'd been in the country for about five or six months, and I got a letter from my brother. "Hey, bro. I've got good news and bad news. I know you like bad news first, so you just got drafted. Good news! You're about half done!" Wow, I was right. Tactics started to change, and we were losing people left and right. I knew then, like I knew before, that my timing was everything.

Chapter 36

Sometime back in 2021, I was shopping at the IGA in Kinsman, Ohio, as I usually did, and I was talking with Bill Weiss, the butcher. If you know me, you know that I like to chat. I don't have to know you, but I will over time. I was telling Bill about Dee's cancer, how hard it was on her and me, and all we were going through. At one point, he and his wife, Branda, grabbed my hands and started praying for Dee and me. I didn't know if that was okay per store policy, but no one put up a fuss. I felt honored that Bill would do that and energized because he did. The next week, Bill gave me a book titled *10 Hours to Live* by Brian Wills. What a story! Brian was a young man in his twenties who was diagnosed with Burkitt's lymphoma, a kind of cancer. No one had ever survived this terrible disease. His story told how he and his parents read healing scriptures for six months while he went through chemo treatments, and he survived. They said he'd never walk again. He ended up playing semipro tennis and went on to teach it for another ten years. They said he'd never be able to have kids. He has four grown and very healthy children. Bill told me that Brian was coming here shortly and wanted to come over and meet us. I didn't know what to say. I almost asked if he had the right guy. I was excited. I didn't know what to expect, but I was really looking forward to it. I had to keep telling myself that it wasn't Jesus who was coming over. He was just a man with a phenomenal story. That day came a few weeks later, and we spent the evening talking, sharing stories, and praying. Dee and I both felt energized. It felt like we'd known each other for years. We were with many people who had nothing but positive thoughts.

I had made friends with a couple of people who worked at the local dollar store. Their mom had cancer also, and they could tell the same story I could. I felt like I had this nice little support group, and we were finding the good in others. Having had anger issues most of my life, you could imagine what a blessing it was to have met so many really good people—good, God-fearing Christians.

Sometime later, Bill told me that he had a surprise for Dee and me and that he and Brenda would pick us up and take us home whenever Dee had enough. I didn't have a clue what it was, but I knew Bill well enough to know that whatever he had planned was a good thing. He and Brenda picked us up, and we went back to Kinsman and took the road east from town square. The land was mostly ranches and wide open, and it went up a rolling hill to where our surprise was. It was just getting dark, and as we approached the top of the hill, we saw a thirty-seven-foot white cross that had just lit up. It was gorgeous. We got to the house and met Tim and Susan Tricker, the owners and architects of the cross. We spent four hours with them that evening, and we couldn't have felt more welcome. It felt like we'd known them for years. Tim played his guitar, and Susan sang some songs. Diane and I were getting out with good people now and really enjoying ourselves.

I had been reading the Bible for about a year and learning more every day. I read the whole book first, then went back and picked out a scripture that was pertinent to what I wanted to learn. There was so much I didn't know, and I wanted to soak it all up.

A few weeks later, Bill brought over another friend who was interested in page one of the Bible, like I was. He thought we could discuss the topic, share some stories, and listen to some guitar music. It was another enlightening experience. I enjoyed discussing the subject matter we could only have an opinion of and never really know for sure with like-minded people. I was tired of everyone else's interpretation of the Bible and wanted to learn as much as I could, so I could make up my own mind. I never liked being told what to think in the first place. What I know is that it helps me in many ways and supports me amidst confusing times. Our lives have a purpose. Our job is to find out what that purpose is.

Chapter 37

The summer of 2022 brought about a different gardening strategy. I have gardened most of my life since I was a young boy. I love growing things and making good use of the produce. The front of the house, where the garden is, gets limited sunlight—not enough for the plants to be fully productive. I had a couple of trees cut down the year before, but it wasn't enough. I got my neighbor to cut down seven trees in the backyard, and that increased the total sunlight to eleven hours a day. I turned the front yard garden into a strictly raspberry garden. They are very productive there. I laid out wooden pallets in the backyard and used five- and two-gallon buckets for the plants. I used new potting soil and grew tomatoes, green beans, cucumbers, peppers, and marigolds. Marigolds help keep the bugs away. The crop was the best I had in years, and the canning was the most I had done ever. I buy sweet corn and blueberries directly from local farmers, and we stock up for the year. It was especially good to keep busy while Diane was going through her cancer treatments.

Kim, Dee's oldest daughter, had a great idea to build a pergola on the deck, so we could all sit out there comfortably during the summer months. We had put up three canopies in recent years and lost them all to high winds and heavy rain. This pergola was made of steel, so it wasn't going anywhere, ever. The family project was a success, and we all had a good time. It's still there.

2023 was an interesting gardening year because I wanted to grow and can more than ever before, so I could give more away. Unfortunately, there was a woodchuck in the yard that destroyed all my green beans, half of my tomatoes, and all the zucchini. I had no idea what to do, and on top of that, my corn farmer was no longer selling corn locally. The more I read the Bible and learned how to pray, the more giving and forgiving I became. Brian was a big help, teaching me how to pray specifically for what I need and want. Who knew, right? All the new friends we'd been making knew. I was having a hard time with a phone that wouldn't work. Money was being charged to my account that I didn't approve of or know about. I was struggling with the VA as always, and I didn't want to lose the progress I'd been making with anger issues. I had a long talk with Brian, and he told me this. Pray to God and do these four things. Thank God for all he does for me. Tell the devil to keep his hands off my finances, health, phone, crops, and family. Set my angels forth to do my bidding. And it is important to tithe. He said that with all the progress I was making by reading the Bible and learning new ways, the devil was really unhappy with me and doing his best to mess me up. It turns out that praying is very important, and Jesus said, "Ask for what you want and need through me, and you shall receive it." I sure wish I'd learned that much sooner, but I was extremely grateful to be learning it now.

I did what Brian said, and I started to see results in a very short time. Bill picked me up one day and took me to his brother-in-law's farm. He gave us all the tomatoes we could carry. We came back with about ten five-gallon buckets full of big, ripe tomatoes. Then he introduced me to Red Basket Farms here locally, and they got me my normal supply of sweet corn that was every bit as good as the farmer I'd been getting from for eight years. They also got me a huge box of green beans, freshly picked the day before. I got my phone fixed, and I resolved the problems with the VA, so I could continue to get treated and get my defibrillator replaced with a new one. My prayers were answered. I called Brian and told him that I wanted to know who he knew. He said, "You already do, Ken."

Chapter 38

Since I have been reading the Bible, meeting extraordinary people, and learning all I can, my health has improved. I am slow to anger, and I continue to improve on that. I am much more forgiving. I don't curse nearly as much, and I feel bad when I mess up and blurt something out. I do not take the Lord's name in vain anymore. I memorized Psalm 23, the ten commandments, and the full armor of God. I especially like Psalm 91 because that was my story in Vietnam. God saved me. Jesus walked with me. I am so touched by those words that I take them both everywhere I go. I put on the full armor of God every time I go out. I ask for my favorite parking spot when I go to the IGA and an empty pump when I go for gas, so I don't have to wait. What I am learning is awesome, and I get what I ask for. I learned that it's important to have a relationship with God and Jesus, and it is the best thing I have ever applied in my life.

I have believed in God all my life. Although we read the Bible after family dinner when I was growing up, I didn't really understand it. I believed unconditionally, you could say. I honored my parents. I didn't know that it was a commandment. I just trusted them. They divorced when I was young, maybe eight years old, and Bible reading after dinner didn't occur anymore. We still went to church, just not with Dad. He cheated on my mom, and there was a lot of arguing and yelling, and I felt caught in the middle. One day, I was halfway down the stairs with Mom at the top and Dad at the bottom. The yelling and screaming scared me. I had nowhere to go. A couple of years went by, and Mom remarried. We moved into their house, and it was hard leaving home. It was only two blocks away, so school and church remained the same. What didn't work was having four stepsiblings who did not like the change at all. Mom and Pop loved each other very much. I was happy about that, but Pop made it clear that I was not his son. Mom changed her last name, and I thought I was supposed to as well. When I asked, I was told a resounding no by Pop.

I didn't feel like I belonged anywhere. All the Fagel relatives lived in New York, so I had nowhere else I could go for support. I became angry at that point, and it continued over the years. I fought a lot in high school. I tried out for football in the tenth grade and went to practice all summer. The coach refused to give me a uniform, hoping I'd quit. The season began, and I got a uniform but was never put into a game, not even for one play. I never quit. I became really angry at this point, and I felt very isolated. After Vietnam, my anger was at a whole different level. I really knew how to fight. I prayed with a chaplain when I first got to Nam and asked God to protect me, not let me get wounded, and help me get home safely. I was the only man in my unit who never got wounded, and I got home safely. My prayers were answered.

After three divorces, I was in ridiculous pain from all the losses in my life. I still believed in God. I didn't blame him for anything, but I didn't talk to him much. After I got congestive heart failure, I started to change my life, but I was still angry and still didn't talk to God much. I led a much better life after Diane and I moved to Williamsfield together, but I was still quick to anger. After Diane got sick, it humbled me. I picked up my Bible from the 50s and started reading. The print was so small. I could barely read it, so I got a new one with large type. It took me ten months to read it, and I learned quite a bit, but I had even more questions then. Good people were brought into my life, and I started talking to God and Jesus. I asked to be forgiven. I asked for strength, wisdom, and calmness. I asked God to help me be slow in my anger. I started forgiving every-body, and that was hard. I needed a better understanding as to why I should do that. I began to see that it was for my sake more than anything. I then had good people in my life I could ask questions to, and I listened and learned. I used to be a really happy kid, and I wanted that guy back. I had a second-grade teacher who told me one day not to ever stop smiling. She said I had a great smile. I wanted it back. Recently, a friend looked at me and said, "Ken, your face is much softer these days." Wow, I was doing something right for the first time in a long time.

I love life; it's very precious. I want people to love me. I want people to be in my life. I once told a friend that if you are with a woman who has five daughters, it had better be for honorable intentions. I earned the respect of those five daughters in part because of how I treated and took care of their mom. This is my family now, and I love every one of them, as well as the grandkids. I thank God for being patient with me and never giving up on me. I thank Jesus for saving me, healing me, and helping me become a better man. It's been a long journey getting here, and I have a long way to go yet. There, but for the grace of God, I go. Having faith means believing in something you can't see and can't prove. If you have faith, you don't have to see or prove it. It's in your heart, and it's been there since the day God created you. For those who don't believe or have faith, God is in your heart. You can deny his existence, and he is still in your heart. You can sin your whole life and still be saved because God has always been in your heart. God works in you; God works for you; and God works through you. You are never alone, even if you think you are. It's important to lead by example and pass these lessons down to our children and grandchildren. Never give up. Never stop praying. Never lose your faith. Never let hate or anger rule your life. All the answers are right there in the Bible. Keep reading, keep learning, and keep asking questions. May God love you and keep you all the days of your life. God bless you all.

My mother loved the hymn "Amazing Grace." I was once lost, but now I'm found.

K. E. Fagel

About the Author

Ken lives in the country by a beautiful lake full of fish, surrounded by a lot of very productive land. He loves to fish, ride horses, garden, produce, canning, read, and play with his grandchildren. He is a seventy-three-year-old Vietnam veteran who served in the 101st Airborne Rangers for one year, and he was the only man not wounded. He thanks God for that. He loves family get-togethers and looks forward to them with excitement. They go on an annual fishing trip and spend the day in the sun, finding good spots to catch. They are blessed with a healthy eagle population that also loves to fish. He especially likes teaching the kids about some of the wonders of the world. He grew up camping, fishing, and learning how to survive outside. He also loves swimming. He spends a lot of time now reading the Bible and learning as much as he can. He has met several people who know quite a bit more than him, so he asks them many questions. It's an important part of how he got here.